Vampires:
Do They Exist?

GAIL B. STEWART

San Diego, CA

For more information, contact:
ReferencePoint Press, Inc.
PO Box 27779
San Diego, CA 92198
www.ReferencePointPress.com

Picture credits:
Cover: Dreamstime
AP Images: 17, 27, 43
Fortean: 50, 53
iStockphoto.com: 7, 31
Photofest.com: 62, 71
Photoshot: 66
Science Photo Library: 48

Series design and book layout:
Amy Stirnkorb

LIBRARY OF CONGRESS CATALOGING-IN-PUBLICATION DATA

Stewart, Gail B. (Gail Barbara), 1949-
  Vampires: Do they exist? / by Gail B. Stewart.
      p. cm. -- (Vampire library series)
  Includes bibliographical references and index.
  ISBN-13: 978-1-60152-110-1 (hardback)
  ISBN-10: 1-60152-110-3 (hardback)
  1. Vampires. I. Title.
  BF1556.S78 2010
  001.944--dc22

                                                                200904312

Contents

Introduction: Mercy's Grave   4

Chapter 1: Why Do People Believe in Vampires?   9

Chapter 2: Close Encounters   24

Chapter 3: Blood and Guts   40

Chapter 4: Vampires Among Us   56

Source Notes   73

For Further Exploration   75

Index   76

About the Author   80

Mercy's Grave

The year 1892 brought many new and exciting advances to the world. Astronomers for the first time used powerful new telescopes to study gigantic, faraway clouds called novas. French engineer Rudolf Diesel invented a revolutionary new engine that even in the twenty-first century still bears his name. And in Buenos Aires, Argentina, police opened the world's first fingerprint bureau, using the tool that would revolutionize the war against crime.

But at the same time that the world was edging toward the twentieth century with inventions and progress in virtually every field, a strange event was occurring in a little town in southern Rhode Island called Exeter. It happened in the cold, dark hours before dawn on March 17, 1892. A small group of men gathered in the local cemetery. Their mission was to find—and destroy—a vampire.

"Dreadful Dreams"

This event actually began because of the strange circumstances surrounding the deaths in the family of George Brown, a local farmer. His wife, Mary, who had always enjoyed perfect health, came down with a mysterious illness in the winter of 1883 and very quickly died. The following spring their daughter Mary Olive began to show similar symptoms—a high fever and a cough. According to historian and folklorist Bob Curran, Mary Olive experienced trouble breathing, especially at night. "She complained of dreadful dreams," Curran writes, "and was vaguely aware of a crushing weight upon her chest as she slept. She grew pale and haggard, and, as summer came in, she began to fade more quickly."[1] Like her mother, Mary Olive died quickly, with her family helpless to do anything about it.

Several years after Mary Olive's death, her brother Edwin—a newlywed who lived with his wife in a nearby village—came down with the same illness. Edwin, too, reported feeling that it was impossible to breathe. Like his older sister, he experienced the crushing sensation in his chest and, even more frightening, said he felt there was a strange presence with him in the bedroom. He also told the local doctor that he was so tired it was as if he no longer had any blood in his body. As Edwin battled his illness, he got word that his 19-year-old sister, Mercy, had just died from the same mysterious condition that had claimed his mother and his other sister.

The Return to Folk Medicine

Doctors had no idea what was causing the disease, and as a result, no idea of how to treat it. Edwin was failing fast, and the medical treatments they were trying had little effect. Desperate and worried about how many more mysterious deaths there would be, elders of the communities of Exeter and nearby Wickford came to Edwin's bedside. They discussed other deaths that had occurred in the area more than a century before and how citizens then had taken drastic steps to stop the spread of that disease.

Edwin listened as they talked about folktales in which an evil presence stalked the rural areas of Rhode Island, taking

Strange as It Sounds...

Stories about vampire-like creatures can be found in the folklore of more than 70 cultures worldwide.

the blood from victims and leaving them so ill and weak that they died soon after. The elders suggested that since science was not working, it was perhaps time to try something more radical—something that would drive the evil presence away.

An article in the *Providence Journal* on March 19, 1892, reported on the weight the folktales carried among the town elders. According to those tales, the culprit was probably someone who had died and then somehow returned to the living world. "[The elders] expressed implicit faith in the old theory that by some unexplained and unreasonable way in some part of the deceased relative's body live flesh and blood might be found."[2]

The elders sought George's permission to dig up the bodies of his dead wife and children in hopes of discovering a blood trail that would lay the mystery to rest. He granted the request, and the next night they gathered at the cemetery for the exhumation.

"Mercy Lay as If She Were Asleep"

Harold Metcalf, a local doctor who had some experience in surgery, led the group. Though weak and ill, Edwin Brown accompanied them. They first went to the graves of Edwin's mother and sister Mary Olive, and with Edwin's consent, they opened the caskets and inspected them. They found skeletal remains but no evidence of fresh blood.

Metcalf then turned his attention to Edwin's younger sister, Mercy, who had been dead only nine weeks. Because Mercy had died in the winter when the frozen ground made it difficult to dig a grave, her body had been placed in a small crypt, where it was to lie until spring. The men gathered around the casket as Metcalf opened it and were horrified to see that she looked almost alive. Curran writes: "After nine

weeks there should have been some visible trace of decomposition, but there was none. Mercy lay as if she were asleep, her skin slightly ruddy in the torchlight, and around the edges of her mouth were the faintest traces of blood."[3]

Convinced that he had found the vampire who had killed the others, Metcalf used his scalpel to cut out her heart and liver, placed them in a remote corner of the cemetery, and burned them. Metcalf and the village elders believed that burning the organs would stop any further vampire activity and protect the community. No one knows for certain whether their actions had the desired effect.

Strong Beliefs

Though many people of the twenty-first century think of vampires as a good subject for horror movies or popular novels, relatively few believe they ever existed. However, the story above is not folklore or legend—it actually happened. In the late nineteenth century, people in Exeter and elsewhere strongly believed in the existence of beings that rose from the grave to attack the living.

People in some parts of the world still believe in the existence of vampires. Some point to stories about vampires throughout history and say that no one has ever been able to prove that those stories were fabricated. So who is to say that similar creatures do not exist today?

Chapter 1

Why Do People Believe in Vampires?

For thousands of years people have been telling stories about ghosts, monsters, and other frightening beings. None of these is likely to terrorize listeners as much as the vampire, a creature who leaves its grave to attack and ultimately kill innocent people. In its wake it leaves victims who are often doomed to become vampires themselves.

Many in the twenty-first century do not know that there was a time when belief in vampires was strong and unwavering. They do not realize that for many people long ago, the question was not whether vampires existed, but rather, when the next vampire would strike.

They Are Everywhere

One reason for the long-running belief in vampires is folklore. In almost every civilization throughout history, in every culture, people have grown up hearing stories about vampires. They were not always known by the term *vampires*; in fact, the first known use of that word did not occur before the 1600s. But many of these creatures shared certain characteristics that are attributed to vampires—the fact that they were dead, but did not stay dead, and that they could survive only by making trouble for the living, which often meant attacking or killing them.

In ancient Bolivia there was the *abchanchu*, a vampire who seemed like a shy, somewhat forgetful, but kind old man. When he approached unsuspecting people to ask directions, the *abchanchu* killed them by biting them and sucking every drop of blood from their bodies.

The ancient Greeks believed in a vampire called Lamia, who had the upper body and head of a woman and the lower body of a large snake. Lamia was one of the many lovers of Zeus, the king of all the Greek gods. Lamia bore several children from her affair with Zeus, and when his wife, Hera, found out, she stole the children. Angry because she was not powerful enough to fight Hera, Lamia took her revenge on human children throughout Greece, sucking their blood until they died.

Another vampire was greatly feared by the Malaysian people of long ago. Called the *penanggalan*, it targeted young children, just as Lamia did. Malaysians believed this vampire was created when a man mistakenly walked in on an ancient religious ceremony meant only for women. A woman who was preparing for the ceremony was so startled to see a man in the room with her that she moved abruptly to get away, and in doing so, her head separated from the rest of her body.

As a result of this accident, she became an angry *penanggalan*. This vampire consisted only of a head with glistening

Keeping a Vampire Busy

One little-known trait of vampires, according to those who hunted the creatures long ago, is their need to count things over and over again. This need afforded villagers a means of protecting themselves and possibly preventing future vampire attacks. Vampire hunters sometimes urged people to place piles of seeds, sand, or small stones near the graves of suspected vampires. If a vampire rose from one of those graves, it would see the piles and feel compelled to count every single seed, sand grain, or stone. The vampire would become so engrossed in this task, the thinking went, that it would never leave the cemetery.

intestines hanging from it, but it caused great problems in villages throughout Malaysia. It perched on the rooftops of homes where children were being born. Screeching, it would try to enter the home so it could suck the blood of the new-born babies.

The Inner Vampire

Folktales such as these present many different ideas concerning the origins of vampires. The ancient Chinese had an altogether different view of the transformation from human to vampire. They believed that every person had the capability to become a *chiang-shi*, or vampire. According to this belief, every human being had two parts to his or her soul. One, the *hun*, was considered the superior part of the soul. It was the more rational, reasonable side. The *p'ai* was more emotional, more prone to acting without thinking things through. And if the *p'ai* remained inside a person's dead body, it could possibly turn that body into a vampire.

It was impossible to tell whether the *p'ai* controlled the body of the deceased at the time of death. But within hours after death, terrifying things would begin to happen. Some of these changes were physical. The *chiang-shi* would grow long fangs with knife-sharp edges. Its eyes would turn blood-red.

According to Chinese folklore, there was—luckily—a limit to the power of the *p'ai.* Once a body had been buried, even a strong *p'ai* was not capable of giving the body strength to rise out of the ground. The belief in the *chiang-shi* was part of the reason Chinese burials occurred quickly after death.

"The Man Who Was Buried Three Times"

Many of the scariest tales concern real people who were said to have transformed into vampires after death. One of these was Abhartach, who was a much-feared chieftain and ruler

Strange as It Sounds

In the folklore of eastern Europe, a corpse with a left eye that did not stay closed marked a person as a vampire.

in fifth-century Ireland. Abhartach was notorious for his cruelty, not only to enemy soldiers, but to his own subjects, who wanted to get rid of him. The people of his kingdom were too frightened of him to attempt killing him, however, so they persuaded a warrior named Cathain to do it.

When Cathain killed him, he buried Abhartach according to the custom for kings or warriors of the time—in an upright position. The day after his funeral, however, villagers saw Abhartach walking among his subjects, demanding that they slit their wrists into a bowl so that he could drink their blood. Horrified, the people of the kingdom contacted Cathain and demanded he return to kill Abhartach once more. Again he was killed and buried, and again he came back from the grave demanding blood.

Finally, Cathain consulted a magician, who advised him to use a sword made from the wood of a yew tree. Yews have long been considered good luck in helping the dead move easily to the afterlife. In addition, Cathain was told to bury Abhartach upside down and sprinkle thorns around the grave site. The magician also told him to place a heavy rock directly over the grave so the body could not rise again. Cathain did as he was instructed, putting a stone monument above the grave. The vampire never returned.

Folklorist Bob Curran reports:

> Today the [monument] is gone, although it is said that one massive capstone remains over the actual burial site. A tree has grown there, too—supposedly from the original thorns. . . . The land is considered "bad ground" and has changed ownership several times, and few locals will approach the place after dark, even

today. In the region they still talk about "the man who was buried three times."[4]

Everyday Vampire Advice

Folktales were not the only way people heard about vampires over the years. Vampires were so commonly discussed in some cultures that elders used them to explain everyday events. The following example, found by researcher Agnes Murgoci, is a story Romanian elders long ago would tell if a child wanted to know why people say "bless you" (or in this case, "good health") after someone sneezes.

The story began as a young noble was getting ready to start on a journey. His horse was saddled and waiting outside the house, but there was a thief creeping close, intending to steal the noble's horse. Murgoci writes:

> As [the thief] came near, he saw a vampire just under the window, waiting for an opportunity to put a spell on the noble. The noble sneezed, and quickly the thief said, "Good health," for if he had not done so the vampire would have seized the occasion to bewitch the noble, and he would have died. It was, however, the vampire who burst with anger at missing his chance.[5]

As people came outside to see what all the commotion was about, the thief showed them the gruesome sight—the burst body of the vampire. When they realized what had happened, the parents of the young noble were very grateful to the thief, and as a reward, gave him the horse he had intended to steal. According to the story, "This shows us that we must always say, 'Good health' when anyone sneezes."[6]

Explaining the Unexplainable

Another important reason why people believed in the existence of vampires was that they provided an explanation for things that were frightening, confusing, or unexplainable. When crops failed, sudden illness claimed a life, or a baby was born dead or deformed, ancient peoples had no way of knowing the causes of these disturbing events. They could only assume that supernatural forces had robbed them of the people they loved or things they needed for survival. And this was the signature of the vampire—a being who, for whatever reason, was the cause of bad luck. In addition to drinking blood, a vampire could make rain stop falling, crops die, herds of animals get sick, and even a new baby die.

This reasoning led the elders in Edwin Brown's community to dig up the graves of his sisters and mother in 1892. In actuality, they had died of tuberculosis, a very contagious disease that was not well understood at that time. And though it sounds strange in the twenty-first century, historians say it was far more comforting for victims and their families to have a supernatural cause, such as a vampire, than to be completely baffled by such events.

No one knew about the existence of germs before the invention of the microscope, which was not invented until after 1600. And, says history researcher Ray Bhirk, even if people had heard of germs causing disease, it would hardly have been accepted as an explanation:

> People forget that the knowledge about germs causing disease is a relatively recent thing. So telling [people] that they were sick because of things that they can't see that are getting into their bodies through their nose or mouth—

Strange as it Sounds...

People in fifteenth- and sixteenth-century India used to carry a charm made of lead to ward off vampire attacks.

that would have been far less believable than a vampire causing the disease. It's easy to see why so many people centuries ago made the connection with a curse or another supernatural cause for their troubles. A vampire was an answer, which to them was better than having no answer. Plus, it was an answer their parents had had, and their grandparents before them, so there was comfort in that.[7]

"By Its Pestiferous Breath"

William of Newburgh was a chronicler who kept track of events and trends in England during the twelfth century. In his book *History of the Events of England*, he details an account of how vampires were able to cause plague—an especially contagious and deadly form of illness. In one story of a vampire from York, the disease spread through the creature's terrible stench rather than through his bite.

This particular story is about an unnamed man from York who led a criminal life and became a vampire when he died. According to William, the creature rose "from his grave at night-time, and pursued by a pack of dogs with horrible barkings, he wandered through the courts and around the houses."[8]

Tales of the vampire spread throughout the town, William says, and people frantically took precautions. He writes:

> All men made fast their doors and did not dare to go [outside] on any errand whatever from the beginning of the night until the sunrise, for fear of meeting and being beaten black and blue by this vagrant monster. But

Vampire-killing techniques passed from one generation to the next. Pictured is a vampire-killing kit from nineteenth-century England. It includes a pistol, silver bullets, a cross, and vials of herbs and potions to ward off the undead.

those precautions were of no avail, for the atmosphere, poisoned by the [smell] of this foul carcass, filled every house with disease and death by its pestiferous breath.[9]

Indeed, William explains, so many people died from the horrible smell of the vampire's body and breath that the town, "which but a short time ago was populous, appeared almost deserted; while those of its inhabitants who had escaped destruction migrated to another part of the country, lest they, too, should die."[10]

Doing Away with Vampires

The belief in vampires was reinforced by the many methods devised for doing away with them. For example, the acts of burning body parts or driving a stake through the vampire's heart were widely known methods for killing vampires. These and other techniques passed from generation to generation, in effect confirming the existence of the creatures for whom they were intended.

In the case of the York vampire, impatient townspeople decided to take matters into their own hands. They nervously went to the cemetery where the man was buried. They were ready to dig him up, believing that he was deep in his grave; however, they were alarmed when they saw that the body was just below the surface.

They realized at once, William explained, that this was indeed the body of a vampire. It was "gorged and swollen with frightful corpulence, and its face was florid and bloated, with huge red puffed cheeks." One member of the crowd struck the corpse with a sharp shovel, and out of the body "flowed such a stream of blood, that it might have been taken for a leech filled with the blood of many persons."[11] They then dragged the body to a large bonfire and, after repeatedly striking it with the shovel, tore out its heart and burned the body until nothing but ash was left.

Shovels, Horses, and Irons

In many regions of the world, specialized vampire hunters earned a living locating corpses suspected of rising from their graves to attack the living. In parts of eastern Europe these vampire hunters were known as *dhampirs*. The *dhampir* was believed to be the son of a woman and her vampire husband. For some reason, although he was the son of a vampire, the *dhampir* did not become a vampire himself, but he was capable of thinking like one. Using his special powers, the *dhampir* was capable of locating vampires whom others could not even see.

Sometimes the *dhampir* was asked to find the identity of a vampire, such as when a witness claimed to have seen but not recognized a vampire. In cases like this, the *dhampir* had a special method. He might ask the citizens if he could borrow a white horse that had never stumbled or a black horse that did not have a single white hair on its body. Then he asked for a young boy or girl to sit on the horse while he led the animal into the cemetery. According to legend, a purely black or white horse with a young child on its back cannot walk over the grave of a vampire. As the *dhampir* led the horse through the cemetery, he soon found a grave that the horse refused to step over.

Whether or not the identity of a vampire was known, the methods of destroying it were the same. Often the *dhampir* would pound a sharp stake into the vampire's body to prevent it from leaving the grave. If a vampire escaped even after this action, the *dhampir* might mutilate the corpse by chopping

"A Wolf Is Born onto the Earth"

It was once believed that a baby born with the caul, or amniotic membrane, still covering it was at great risk of becoming a vampire. It was only by quick action that such a curse could be avoided. In the folklore of Romania, for example, when a baby was born with a caul, it was crucial for the midwife to remove the caul quickly and take the newborn outside. Then, according to vampire researcher Rosemary Ellen Guiley, she called out: "Hear, everyone, a wolf is born onto the earth. It is not a wolf that will eat people, but a wolf that will work and bring luck." By doing this the midwife assured that the caul was not a curse to bring evil, so the child would not be shunned by his or her community.

Quoted in Rosemary Ellen Guiley, *The Encyclopedia of Vampires, Werewolves, and Other Monsters.* New York: Checkmark, 2005, p. 60.

off its head and arms or cutting the large muscles in its legs. Often the body was set on fire or scalded with a red-hot iron. Such methods were almost sure to keep even the most evil and determined vampire from returning to the living.

The Church and Vampires

The familiar routines used to hunt and kill vampires served as proof to many people that such creatures existed. But there was an even stronger reason for people to believe in the existence of vampires—the Christian Church. In the early years of Christianity—especially the twelfth and thirteenth centuries—people's belief that evil demons roamed the Earth was very strong. This was true everywhere but was far more prevalent in some of the more remote areas into which the church was expanding, such as hilly sections of eastern Europe and isolated villages in Ireland, Scotland, and western Europe.

In these places the belief in vampires was firmly entrenched, and this presented a problem for church officials. They did not want to contend with the stories of bloodthirsty vampires when spreading their message about God and salvation. In 1215 Pope Innocent III convened an important meeting of church leaders in Rome, called the Fourth Lateran Council. There were more than 1,000 men in attendance, from powerful city bishops to country priors and abbots.

When missionaries told church officials about the number of incidents supposedly involving vampires in these remote areas, officials agreed that instead of trying to convince people that there was no such thing as vampires, they would have more luck in recognizing the existence of such creatures. In a famous pronouncement (written in Latin, as was the tradition) the council voted to officially recognize the existence of demons and vampires, saying, *"Diabolus enim et alii a Deo quidem natura creati sunt boni, sed ipsi per se facti sunt mali."* In English, that means, "The Devil and the other demons were created by God good in their nature but they by themselves have made themselves evil."[12] From that time on, church officials stressed that the church was the only entity that was powerful enough to defeat vampires. By recognizing that vampires existed, the church demonstrated how important it was in the life of the people who so feared them. People in these rural areas now had a new ally in the fight against vampires.

Predictions of Vampirism

In addition to adding some tools to fight vampires, the church also helped delineate some of the most important signs that a person might become a vampire. Regional folklore throughout western and eastern Europe was already brimming with advice on ways to predict who could likely come back from the grave to cause trouble.

For example, people had believed for centuries that anyone who was born with a deformity such as a cleft palate, a hunched back, or crossed eyes would be very likely to become vampires after they died. There is a story about a young Romanian boy who had been born with one leg much shorter than the other and who, as an infant, was greatly feared by the people of his village. They were certain that he had been cursed and therefore would become a vampire when he died.

People born with noticeably different skin tone or hair color different than others of their region were also believed to be likely vampire candidates. In Greece, for example, where most people had dark hair and brown eyes, a redheaded or blond child with blue eyes would be viewed with suspicion and even fear that he or she would become a vampire.

But the church offered explanations for vampirism, too. One was improper burial without Christian prayers and a priest in attendance. The church taught that one night each year, the dead were permitted to return to the living world. This was on October 31, what is now called Halloween— the night before All Saints' Day. People who did not receive proper Christian burial might take revenge against their living relatives. The idea of a vengeful corpse, say historians, played right into the fears people already had about vampires rising from their graves. This was profitable for the church, too, for many people were more than willing to pay a priest to officiate at burials.

One of the most serious predictors of vampirism the church taught was excommunication, or being expelled from the church. If a person constantly violated Christian teaching, he or she would be officially excommunicated—usually by the local bishop. In the Greek Orthodox Church, it was taught that excommunicated people would not decompose when they were buried, so they could not go to the afterlife. Instead, they would stay fresh and lifelike in the grave for all eternity. In fact, the final line of the excommunication ceremony was, "After death, let not thy body have power to dissolve."[13]

Community elders and folklore supported the belief in vampires. But when the powerful Christian Church attested to the existence of vampires and even became involved in the discussion of how to predict or deal with them, this added a great deal of strength to people's beliefs in these frightening creatures. In fact, the question was no longer one of *why* people believed in vampires, but rather, why would they not?

Chapter 2

Close Encounters

Many of the beliefs that had once seemed very real to people were less plausible as the years went on. Many of the demons and fairies, the trolls and ogres, became relegated to scary stories or children's fairy tales. However, the belief in vampires remained strong, possibly because so many people claimed to have had personal encounters with vampires.

Eventually, it seemed that in almost every town and village in Europe—especially eastern Europe—there were people who claimed to have seen vampires with their own eyes. And they were anxious to tell their tales to anyone who would listen.

The Power of a Pardon

William of Newburgh chronicled a story that took place in Buckinghamshire, in the south of England. A man there had died, but the night after his burial, he rose from the grave as a vampire and attacked his widow as she lay sleeping. William writes that "he suddenly entered the room where his wife lay . . . and, having awakened her, he not only filled her with the greatest alarm, but almost killed her by leaping upon her with the whole heaviness of his weight."[14]

The same thing happened the following night, after which

the woman begged neighbors to stay with her and protect her. As expected, the vampire returned but was driven away by the neighbors. In the nights that followed, the vampire visited his brothers and other family members, pouncing on them as they slept.

The local priest was frantic, for he did not know what his role should be in this case. He wrote a letter to the bishop, who in turn conferred with church officials. Those officials told the bishop that they had received reports of vampires attacking people in this way throughout England. They advised the priest to burn the body before any more attacks could take place.

Even though the bishop had heard ancient tales of vampires being burned, he found the idea of such action repugnant. Instead, the bishop wrote out a special blessing for the man, pardoning him for all of his sins. He gave the blessing to the priest and told him to open the grave and place it on the chest of the body, over the heart. According to William, the man stayed buried, and the vampire attacks ceased.

Confronting the Cross

The official blessing, or pardon, was not the only thing that the church could offer as a means to halt vampire activity. One story, chronicled by an early historian named Walter Map, showed that the symbol of the cross could be a powerful weapon, too.

The story began—as most vampire stories do—when a certain man died. He was an atheist, a person who did not believe in the existence of God. But soon after he was buried, he became a vampire. Though he did not attack anyone, he was said to be restless—his corpse walked throughout the north of England, chased by anxious crowds each time he was seen.

A Vampire Unearthed

In the spring of 2009, Italian researchers found what they believe are the remains of a woman considered to be a vampire. The body was found on the small island of Lazzaretto Nuovo in Venice, in what was a mass grave for victims of a sixteenth-century plague. So many people died during the plague that there was no time or room to bury people individually, so their bodies were thrown into large pits, covered with lime, and covered with several feet of dirt.

The woman's remains were of special interest, for she had been buried with a brick lodged between her jaws—a custom in those days to prevent a suspected vampire from returning to bite the living. One anthropologist said that this discovery supported the hunch that vampires were often blamed for outbreaks of diseases. "This is the first time that archaeology has succeeded in reconstructing the ritual of exorcism of a vampire," he said. "This helps . . . authenticate how the myth of vampires was born."

Quoted in Daniel Flynn, "Discovery Explains Source of Vampire Myth," *Vancouver (BC) Sun*, March 13, 2009, p. B7.

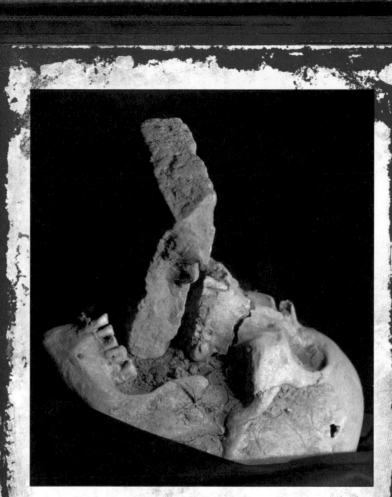

Researchers in Northern Italy uncovered the centuries-old remains of a suspected vampire. According to one ancient ritual, a brick positioned between the vampire's jaws (pictured) would have prevented her from feeding on victims of a plague that swept through Venice in the sixteenth century.

When the vampire stopped roaming, he went back toward his grave but found that the local bishop had erected a cross over it. The cross, writes Map, was too powerful a symbol for the vampire to take on, and so he was unable to get back inside his grave. As the vampire turned to begin roaming again, some men in the crowd removed the cross.

At this, the vampire realized he could finally go back to his grave. As people looked on, the vampire fell inside and covered himself with dirt. Quickly, several of the men raised the cross over the grave again to ensure that the vampire would no longer get out.

Vampire Hysteria

With the church firmly behind the idea of the existence of vampires, it was not surprising that more and more people were feeling brave enough to speak about the vampires they had seen or who had threatened them. In addition, a number of learned people had begun to write books about vampires and their effect on people's lives. One such book was *An Appeal to the Natural Faculties of the Mind of Man*, written in 1653 by Henry More. He asserted that it was an accepted fact that people who committed suicide would return from their graves as vampires.

Another book, *On the Current Opinions of Certain Greeks*, was written in 1645 by a theologian named Leo Allatius. This was the first scholarly book that tackled the subject of vampires. In it Allatius discussed how the church was dealing with vampires and offered theories about their existence and their origins. His book contained accounts of people's experiences with vampires, experiences that Allatius described as true.

One such story involved a vampire on the Greek island of Khíos. This vampire was known to knock on people's doors, and Allatius asserted that anyone who answered the door would be dead by the next morning. The residents dealt with the problem by not answering their doors until they had waited several minutes, because a vampire would never knock twice. Allatius's scholarly approach to such stories validated the idea of vampires roaming the countryside in search of blood.

Respected writers during the seventeenth century such as Allatius and More solidified the idea of vampires being a real threat to people. Partly as a result of such validation, say historians, reports of deaths by blood-sucking demons increased, and people in many parts of Europe were almost hysterical with terror. At the mere suggestion that a villager had died suspiciously, townspeople would rush to the local cemetery to dig up the body. If it had any of the signs of a vampire (fresh blood or lifelike appearance), the body was hacked to pieces and burned.

"Ye Must Summon the Priests"

The hysteria began to worry church officials in Rome. They realized with alarm that they had made a mistake. They had been eager to convert people to Christianity—people who believed strongly in vampires. The church had tapped into that fear and made a decision not only to tell these people that vampires did exist, but also to insist that only through Christianity could vampires be conquered. As a result, they had only fueled the fires of vampire hysteria.

The burning and dismemberment of buried bodies was particularly horrifying to church officials. The church taught that burial was a holy ritual. Exhumation for the purpose of dismembering and burning the corpse went against church teachings. Priests advised the peasants in rural areas to involve the church rather than take matters into their own hands. "When such remains be found," church officials stated, "ye must summon the priests to chant an invocation of the Mother of

God . . . and to perform memorial services for the dead."[15]

But the panic did not stop, and priests were not always consulted in cases of suspected vampire activity. In fact, the hysteria over vampires was becoming an embarrassment for the church, especially because of the link church officials had made between vampirism and excommunication. In a very real way, writes vampire researcher Olga Hoyt, "consigning the body [of an excommunicated person] forever to the realm of the un-dead, meant the Church was creating vampires."[16]

Arnold Paole

By the eighteenth century vampire hysteria had hit an all-time high in eastern and central Europe. In 1731 one very famous vampire incident occurred in Medwegya, Austria. The story centered around a quiet farmer named Arnold Paole, who always seemed to have a cloud of gloom over him. When asked by his wife and friends why he was so depressed, he explained that when he was in the army in Persia he had been bitten by a vampire.

Paole said that he had immediately taken steps to prevent becoming a vampire himself—going to the cemetery and opening the tomb of the vampire who had bitten him, eating some of the dirt from around the grave, and even rubbing some of the blood from that vampire's body on his own. However, he confided, he was often bothered by a feeling that those precautions were not enough and that he still might be doomed to become a vampire when he died.

Though many thought these were merely entertaining stories, they changed their minds after Paole broke his neck falling from a hay wagon on his farm and died. During the following month four other people in the village died suddenly. Remembering Paole's vampire story, people who knew Paole began to suspect that he actually was a vampire and that he had caused these subsequent deaths. As a result,

OPPOSITE:
In many vampire stories the cross is a powerful tool for warding off attacks. In at least one instance, a cross placed on the grave of a suspected vampire prevented the creature from returning to the living world.

a mob of villagers stormed the local cemetery and dug up his grave. As they suspected, Paole's corpse showed what was thought to be the proof of vampirism—hair and nails that were still growing and blood around his mouth.

To kill this vampire the mob drove a sharp stake through his heart and was horrified to hear a loud groan come from the body. This seemed to them irrefutable proof that he was a vampire, and the villagers cut off Paole's head and burned his body. They then moved on to the graves of the four who had died after Paole and did the same to those bodies—hoping to prevent what seemed like a vampire epidemic from spreading further.

"The People . . . Were Beside Themselves"

That should have been the end of the troubles, but four years later, there were 17 more unexplained deaths in the village. All of these occurred within the space of three months, and few of the victims had been battling illness. In fact, most had been young and healthy before dying suddenly. This seemed both odd and frightening to the townspeople. Elders reminded the townspeople about Arnold Paole and his victims and suggested that the evil was still among them. A teenage girl in the village fueled fears when she reported that one of the dead, a young man named Milo, had appeared to her soon after he had died.

The attacks were not aimed only at humans, either. Farmers reported that cattle had been attacked, presumably by vampires who sucked some of their blood. That caused an even greater panic, writes Hoyt:

> It was well known that any person who ate meat from an animal attacked by a vampire, became a vampire. Consequently the people of Medwegya were beside themselves. No family trusted any other; every accident to

any person or animal was now attributed to vampires; slaughtered cattle were left to rot, and the whole social structure of the village was in disarray.[17]

At the Emperor's Request

The terror of Medwegya spread to other villages, and it did not take long for the turmoil to come to the attention of governmental authorities. In December 1731 Regimental Field Surgeon Johannes Fluckinger was given orders from Emperor Charles VI of Austria. "Having heard from various quarters that so-called vampires have been responsible for the death of several persons, by sucking their blood," Fluckinger wrote, "I have been commissioned . . . to throw some light on this question."[18]

Fluckinger patiently interviewed every one of the villagers, trying to understand what had caused the panic. He heard about Arnold Paole and the four people who had died after him. He soon realized that there would be no calm until the latest presumed vampires had been dug up and killed once and for all. Fluckinger supervised as the bodies were disinterred one by one with the help of local soldiers. After each body was dug up, Fluckinger did a crude autopsy to study it and note anything unusual. For instance, a 20-year-old woman named Stana had died in childbirth two months before. Upon opening her body Fluckinger saw a great deal of red blood and recorded that "the lung, liver, stomach, spleen, and intestines were quite fresh as they would be in a healthy person."[19]

The body of a 60-year-old woman who had died of a three-month illness seemed to look quite healthy, too. In fact, Fluckinger noted, "during her dissection, all the [soldiers] who were standing around marveled greatly at her plumpness and perfect body, uniformly stating that they had known the woman well, from her youth, and that she had, throughout her life, looked . . . very lean and dried up."[20]

In his final report to the Austrian government, Fluckinger said that of the 40 bodies dug up, 17 were found to be vampires. They were destroyed according to the local custom, Fluckinger writes: "After the examination had taken place, the heads of the vampires were cut off by the local [people] and burned along with the bodies, and then the ashes were thrown into the River Moravia. The decomposed bodies [those showing no signs of vampirism], however, were laid back into their own graves."[21]

A Change of Heart

Already worried about the growing number of bodies being disinterred, burned, and dismembered, church officials tried to reverse their position—changing their earlier statements that a person excommunicated from the church would not decompose. They now stressed that just because a body had not begun to decompose did not mean that the body was that of a vampire. More importantly, the church appealed to scholars and writers to address the subject of vampirism, as they had centuries before. This time, however, church officials hoped these new books would ease the fear of vampires, rather than whip it up.

One scholar, an Italian archbishop named Giuseppe Davanzati, wrote *A Dissertation on Vampires* in 1744. Davanzati cast doubt on the existence of vampires; he said they were merely fantasies of superstitious, uneducated, rural people. In the book, Davanzati wondered why it was always the lower classes that claimed to have seen vampires, while higher classes of people never did:

Why is this demon so partial to baseborn [common people]? Why is it always peasants, carters, shoemakers, and innkeepers? Why has the demon never been known to assume the form of a man of quality, a scholar, a philosopher, a theologian, a magnate, or a bishop? I will tell you why: learned men and men of quality are not so easily deceived as idiots and men of low birth and therefore do not so easily allow themselves to be taken in by appearances.[22]

A Less Certain View

While Davanzati left no room in his argument for the existence of vampires (except as fantasy), another book published around the same time also by a member of the clergy came to a different conclusion. Dom Augustin Calmet, a French monk and theologian, addressed the subject of vampires in 1746 in a two-volume work whose English title was *The Phantom World.* More than any other book on the subject, Calmet's work—a best-seller in Europe—was responsible for making the word *vampire* (used in Fluckinger's report) a household word among European people. Until then each region and culture had used its own term for the creature.

Calmet's book did more than introduce the term to his many readers. He also took a close look at the number of vampire stories that had been circulating throughout Europe for centuries. Unlike Davanzati, who before writing his book was certain that vampires were nothing more than a myth, Calmet approached it with an open mind.

For example, he questioned why, if a vampire was able to leave its grave and walk among the living, it did not leave footprints in the dirt in the cemetery. Or, he wondered, if the

How to Repel a Vampire

- Using any weapon made of silver will help, since vampires are afraid of it. In addition, one is safe wearing a cross or other religious charm made of silver.

- Two false eyes painted on the forehead of a large black dog will scare away a vampire.

- A cross made from the thorns of wild roses and worn around the neck will also scare away vampires.

- Many people in eastern Europe believed that whitethorn frightens vampires. They say that because Jesus wore a crown of thorns from the whitethorn tree, this tree and its thorns are likely to confuse and disorient a vampire.

- Building a good, bright fire will keep vampires away.

vampire was a spirit, how could it do the damage it did without a flesh-and-blood body? He also suggested that there could be a good reason why most vampires seemed to appear in Serbia, Poland, and other eastern European countries where people were well-known for being superstitious.

Though he did not go so far as to suggest that vampires did exist, he admitted that he could see why so many believed in them:

> We are told that dead men return from their tombs, are heard to speak, walk about, injure both men and animals whose blood they drain, making them sick and finally causing their death. Nor can the men [save] themselves unless they dig the corpses up and drive a sharp stake through their bodies, cut off their heads, tear out their hearts, or else burn the bodies to ashes. It seems impossible not to subscribe to the prevailing belief that these apparitions do actually come forth from their graves.[23]

Because Calmet could not prove that vampires did *not* exist, he refused to make that his conclusion. This set Calmet up for derision; many scholars scoffed at his ideas. However, many who already believed in vampires felt their views had been validated, for such a learned man had taken them seriously and had not been able to prove them wrong.

Exaggeration and Panic

The literary works of Davanzati and Calmet did not have any real effect on halting the vampire hysteria. One of the people most disappointed in this was Empress Maria Theresa of

Austria-Hungary. She was horrified at the stories she had heard of corpses being dug up and destroyed—especially those of young children. At the time, vampire hysteria was raging in Silesia, just east of what is today the Czech Republic.

In 1755 the empress insisted on sending her personal physician, Gerhard van Swieten, to Silesia to investigate. In his report to the empress, he said he believed that it was the church that was whipping the local people into a panic about vampires, and this led to exaggeration about the condition of dead bodies. Van Swieten gave an example of one recent incident:

> One of the vampires "executed" was said to have been swollen with blood, since the executioner, a thoroughly reliable man, no doubt, in matters concerning his trade, claimed that when he cut up bodies which were sentenced to be burned, a great quantity of blood gushed forth. Nevertheless, he afterwards agreed that this great quantity was about a spoonful—and this is a very different matter.[24]

Van Swieten also said that the church's insistence that every tiny detail of a Christian burial be followed, lest the corpse become a vampire, was causing problems. In religious rituals that were so complex, van Swieten reported, it was very easy for someone to look back and note that some small detail had been missed or had been done incorrectly. It was no wonder, he said, that so many vampire executions began with someone claiming that their loved one had not received every aspect of the burial ritual, down to the last letter.

"No One Can Reasonably Doubt Its Validity"

Determined to do away with vampire executions, the empress issued a royal proclamation. From that day forward, any and all vampire outbreaks would be investigated by the government, not the church. In addition, anyone who believed strongly that a dead body was returning and causing problems needed to submit proof to the government before any grave was dug up.

The effect of these laws was not as helpful as Maria Theresa had hoped, for the belief in vampires still remained strong. In fact, one German journalist commented that the evidence of vampires was too convincing for most people to change their minds about it. "[Vampirism] is proved by so many facts," he wrote, "that no one can reasonably doubt its validity, given the quality of the witnesses who have certified the authority of those facts."[25]

By the middle of the eighteenth century, there seemed to be a number of good reasons to believe in vampires. What had begun as numerous vampire legends throughout much of Europe had grown into something more. Not only had the Christian Church recognized the existence of vampires, but there were now laws addressing the existence and effects of vampires—and the correct way to deal with them. It seemed that with the institutions of law, religion, and culture addressing vampirism, it would be hard to convince anyone they were merely superstition—at least, anytime soon.

Chapter 3

Blood and Guts

When vampire hunters and others entered cemeteries to dig up graves, they did so with a purpose. They were searching for suspected vampires. And usually they found them. But what made them so sure the corpse in the grave was truly a vampire? Superstition, folklore, and the absence of any real understanding of science contributed mightily. But science and human behavior can also help to answer this question.

Motionless and Silent but Not Dead

One common thread of many vampire stories is that the disinterred body looks eerily different from its condition at the time of burial. In one case in northern Romania in 1722, for example, a vampire hunter opened a suspected vampire's coffin, and the crowd of onlookers was horrified to see blood on the face and mouth of the body.

They assumed this must be a vampire, for he still bore signs of having drunk the blood of some unfortunate victim the night before. Even more damning, the body had moved in its coffin since being buried—the hands were up by the head, not clasped on the chest, as was the custom then. As frightening as this likely was for the villagers who accompanied the vampire hunter, there is another possible explanation for the body's condition. This explanation is perhaps more horrible than vampirism—that the person was not dead when he was buried.

One way this can happen is if a person has a rare condition called catalepsy. A person who suffers from catalepsy is in what is often called "suspended animation"—he or she seems lifeless but is actually alive. Breathing becomes very slow and difficult to detect—even for a doctor. The muscles stiffen so much that the condition might be mistaken for rigor mortis, which happens naturally after death. Catalepsy is not the same as a coma, for a person with catalepsy is fully awake and aware but is unable to respond. Even the tiny blink of an eyelid is impossible.

A true-life example occurred in London in 1895. A young boy had been found lying motionless on the grass in a city park, and because he did not appear to be breathing and his body was stiff, doctors pronounced him dead. As he lay in the morgue waiting to be processed for burial, he began to show signs of life, reports vampire researcher Olga Hoyt: "Fortunately, the morticians had not begun their grisly work. . . . They called a doctor. By the time a doctor arrived, he was breathing normally. When he was taken to a hospital the medical verdict was that the boy was 'recovering from a fit.' He was lucky enough to live for many years after."[26]

Premature Burial

Similar mistakes have been documented even as recently as the 1920s. About 50 cases per year occurred in Europe and the United States in which a person who was declared dead turned out to be suffering from catalepsy. Luckily many of those came out of their cataleptic state before they were buried.

The likelihood of this happening today is much smaller,

mainly because most parts of the United States have laws that bodies must be embalmed before they are buried. That means that blood is drained from the body and replaced with chemicals that keep it from decaying. Centuries ago embalming was common practice for burial of Egyptian royalty but much less common elsewhere in the world. For the most part, bodies were buried quickly, adding to the possibility of premature burial. People who found themselves in this unfortunate position might have tried to scratch their way out of a coffin, bloodying their hands and faces before they died from thirst or lack of air. Catalepsy may provide an intriguing explanation for *some* vampire stories, but it cannot account for all of them. The explanation for those may be found in other areas of scientific knowledge.

A Plump Corpse

One commonly reported observation by people who attended the disinterment of a suspected vampire was that the body seemed remarkably plump. The plumpness, it was believed, resulted from the drinking of blood and thus provided proof that the corpse was that of a vampire.

This is what happened to Johann Cuntius, a prominent alderman in Silesia (now part of Germany) in 1592. After he died from injuries sustained when a horse kicked him, people reported seeing Cuntius doing terrible things around town. He was supposedly seen killing dogs and goats, strangling town elders, and even staining the altar of the local church with blood. Wondering whether Cuntius might have become a vampire, the townspeople went to the cemetery to have a look at his body. In his book, *Vampires, Burial, and Death*, author Paul Barber includes an account from an eyewitness to the event who reported an astonishing change in

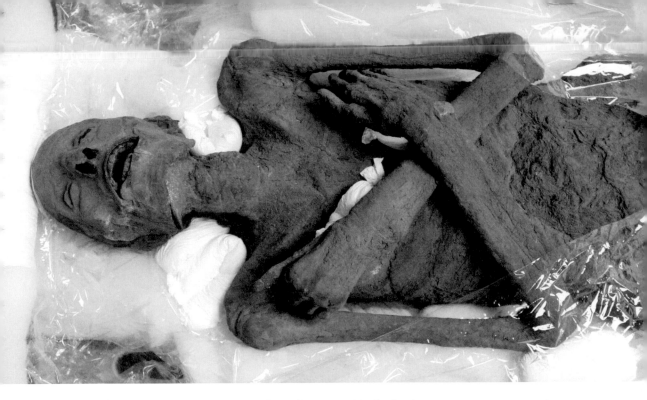

An Egyptian mummy awaits identification. Embalming, a common practice in ancient Egypt, was little known in the rest of the ancient world. Once embalming became more widespread, the likelihood of burying someone alive decreased.

the appearance of Cuntius's body: "[Cuntius] had during life been small in his person, and gaunt, but his corpse was now much sturdier. The face was swollen, the cheeks puffed up, and everything in a vaporous state, much like fattened pigs, so that the bulk of the body hardly had room any more in the coffin, which it had lain in from February 8 to July 20."[27]

It was this plumpness that convinced the townspeople that he was a vampire, for the only explanation they had was that Cuntius had returned from the grave to suck the blood of the living. This probably sounded logical at the time. In the years since then, however, doctors have learned that such changes in the body actually have nothing to do with vampirism.

Understanding Decomposition

Scientists say that decomposition, the gradual breaking down of a body after death, is responsible for many of the suspicious changes people noticed when they opened graves looking for vampires. Decomposition may not be pleasant to think about, but it is an entirely natural part of the life and death process.

When a person dies, his or her body goes through a number of important changes. Bacteria inside multiply, and that creates gases within the body. As the gases increase, the body often swells. Someone who sees a body that has been in the ground for days or weeks might have a hard time recognizing the person they knew in life.

Bodies deteriorate at different rates, depending on the condition of the body when it was buried, the temperature, and the depth of the grave. That means that of two bodies buried at the same time, one might go through such changes in a few days, while the other might take a week or more to begin deteriorating.

"A Great Shriek"

Sometimes this buildup of gases inside the body can have other strange effects. Although Regimental Field Surgeon Johannes Fluckinger was not present when Arnold Paole's body was disinterred and destroyed, he noted in his official report that witnesses had told him "a stake was driven through [Paole's] heart. But as this was being performed, he gave a great shriek and an enormous quantity of blood spurted from the body."[28]

Experts say that the "shriek" was probably nothing more than this buildup of gas escaping quickly as the stake pierced the skin. As the gases escaped, so, too, did other body

Nails, Hair, and Teeth

The unmasking of a vampire often involved the discovery that even in death, the nails, hair, and teeth continued to grow. Or at least they appeared to be growing. When a vampire hunter pried open a coffin, the sight of long fingernails, hair, and even teeth on the corpse seemed certain proof of vampirism. People of centuries ago did not realize they were looking at normal physical changes that accompany death. The hair, fingernails, and teeth were not actually growing, but they appeared to have grown because the rest of the body was changing or shrinking, says anthropologist Paul Barber. "The skin shrinks back as it becomes dehydrated. The toothy appearance of a skull is similar: it does not have longer teeth than it had in life, they are just more evident."

Paul Barber, *Vampires, Burial, and Death: Folklore and Reality.* New Haven, CT: Yale University Press, 1988, p. 119.

fluids—including blood. The spurt of blood, which the frightened onlookers took as proof of a vampire's diet, belonged to the dead man.

Often these gases escape on their own, either suddenly in a burst or gradually. The sound of gas escaping slowly from a corpse is likely the explanation for the vampire hunter's horse. As mentioned earlier, the *dhampir* would lead a horse with a child on its back through the cemetery, looking for the grave of a vampire. It could very well be that the horse, with its acute hearing, could detect the sound of escaping gas coming from the ground. The noise (or the smell) might have spooked the horse, and it would have refused to step over the grave.

The Grave Disturbed?

Finally, there are many cases in which people base their assumption of vampirism on the condition of the grave site. For instance, in 1592 in Hungary a group of citizens went to a cemetery to investigate vampire activity in their town. Upon arrival, they found that the dirt over one of the graves had been disturbed, a possible sign of vampire activity. When they began to dig at the site, they were horrified to find that the body, which had been buried several feet underground, was now just below the surface. They took this as proof that the man had been leaving his grave from time to time to cause trouble in the town.

Interestingly, decomposition can explain this, too. Centuries ago, most bodies were buried in very simple wooden coffins—much different from the heavy, steel-lined caskets used today. Because a wooden coffin was so light, gas from decomposition could actually move it closer to the surface. In some cases the decomposition can even cause part of the body—such as a hand—to emerge from the top of a grave. Such buoyancy of a

Strange as It Sounds...

In the seventeenth and eighteenth centuries, people sometimes buried corpses upside down so that if the body was that of a vampire, it would not be able to find its way to the surface.

decaying body is not limited to humans, either.

Barber cites a story of an Oregon chicken producer who lost thousands of his chickens to heat prostration in 1986. He buried them in a 2-foot-deep (61cm) hole near his driveway. However, 12 hours later, the incredible amount of gas produced by the decomposing chickens buoyed them to the surfaced and actually made the ground crack, spilling the entire mess onto the driveway. "It looked kind of like a lava flow,"[29] one witness said.

True-Life Vampires?

Human behavior, like science, can help explain events that might have kept alive the belief in vampires over such a long span of time. History includes stories of real people whose behavior seemed very much like that of legendary vampires. These were not walking dead, as vampires were believed to be, but instead people who led lifestyles that were ghoulish and cruel. Historians say it is not surprising that the stories about these real-life monsters may have validated the idea of blood-sucking vampires of folklore.

One of those people was a warlord named Vlad, who lived during the fifteenth century in Transylvania, now part of central Romania. He was the son of another Vlad, known as Vlad Dracul, which means "Vlad the devil." Putting an *a* on the end of *Dracul* means "son of the devil," so Vlad became known as Vlad Dracula. And while he was not a blood-drinking creature from beyond the grave, Dracula more than lived up to his name by killing thousands of people. Dracula was what is known as a sadist—a person who derives pleasure from the pain and suffering of others.

His favorite form of torture involved impaling enemies and other people on sharp wooden stakes set into the ground. As

A donated body placed at a staged crime scene allows forensics students in Tennessee to study human decomposition. Ancient peoples often mistook the normal stages of decomposition as evidence of vampires.

Hoyt explains, this was definitely not a private method of execution: "The enemies, men and women, were stripped of their clothes and impaled on spikes in a meadow for everyone to see what happened to those who tried to trick Dracula. The bodies were left in place for many months—eaten by blackbirds and baked by the sun."[30]

Other Cruelties

But impaling was not the only cruelty for which Dracula was known. In fact, it seemed to be almost a point of pride for him to find particularly barbarous methods of inflicting pain on people. One well-known story revolves around a visit from representatives of the Turkish ruler. It was the custom in those days for high-ranking Turks to wear a fez, a flat, cone-shaped hat with a black tassel. It was also the custom not to remove them when indoors, as people did with other types of hats. But when Dracula saw that the three men were not removing their fezzes when coming into his presence, he took that as a sign of disrespect. He ordered his guards to hold each of the three Turks down and had another of his guards nail each man's fez to his head.

In another case, a man had committed robbery in Dracula's district. The man was scheduled to be hanged, but three of his friends came to vouch for him, saying that hanging was not a custom they followed. Dracula agreed to change the punishment. Instead of hanging the thief, he boiled him alive and forced his friends to eat him.

Historians agree that there is no record of his ever drinking a victim's blood. However, it is not hard to imagine that the stories of incredibly cruel men such as Dracula only reinforced people's ideas that angry, bloodthirsty vampires could very well exist. The violent deeds of Dracula made a strong impression on Irish writer Bram Stoker, who used the name for the title character in his famous fiction work, *Dracula*.

Bloody Elizabeth Bathory

Probably no one has come closer to being a real-life vampire than a seventeenth-century Hungarian countess named Elizabeth Bathory. In her life she exhibited as much cruelty as

Strange as It Sounds...

Even though Vlad Dracula was known for exceptional cruelty and bloodlust, Romania issued a series of colorful stamps celebrating the occasion of the five hundredth anniversary of his death.

Vlad, also known as Vlad Dracula, may not have been a blood-drinking creature from the grave but he was clearly evil. In one instance, he is said to have boiled a thief alive and forced the man's friends to eat him.

Vlad Dracula, but with an emphasis on blood—so much so that she was known during her life as the Blood Countess.

Bathory married when she was a teenager. She and her husband, Count Francis Nadasdy of Hungary, chose to set up their home in one of the smaller family castles, a remote place called Csejthe. As Hoyt describes it, Csejthe Castle was a very unsettling, forbidding place: "[It was] a dark and foreboding bastion on a rock high on the side of one of the Carpathian foothills, bordered by dense forests where the wolves howled at night. It was a wild and gloomy place, with thick walls, low ceilings, few windows, and a labyrinth of underground passages, cellars, and dungeons."[31]

Bathory loved her husband and enjoyed having him around, but as time went by, she spent more and more time alone. Nadasdy was a military man, and throughout much of their married life he was busy fighting off Turkish armies attempting to invade the borders of his country. As a result, Bathory often found herself bored and restless in the gloomy Csejthe Castle.

Witchcraft

During this time she learned about witchcraft from several people who worked in her castle. One was Dorko, a nurse who had helped with the rearing of her children. Dorko taught Bathory chants and spells. Many of these had to do with keeping Bathory beautiful, but a few were especially appropriate for dangerous situations. One, which Bathory shared in a letter to her husband during the wars, had to do with keeping him from being harmed by his enemies: "Dorko has taught me something new: Beat a small black fowl to death with a white cane. Put a drop of its blood on your enemy's person, or, if you cannot reach him, on a piece of his clothing. Then he will be unable to harm you."[32]

Another was Darvula, one of her maids who created cosmetic potions for Bathory's skin. Soon Bathory was dabbling in sorcery, too. She was especially interested in preserving her beauty—something she often worried about. Some historians say that she had more than 500 pots and jars of various creams, lotions, and liquids that she used to keep her skin soft.

The Key to Softer Skin

In fact, her obsession with human blood actually began because of her vanity. One of the young servant girls misunderstood Bathory's instructions and brought her something she had not asked for. Angry and impatient, she hit the servant in the face with a pair of scissors, which caused some of the girl's blood to spurt onto her own face. Immediately, say historians, Bathory saw that the skin where the blood had landed was much softer than her other skin.

Excited by what she believed was a breakthrough in her quest for eternally youthful skin, Bathory discussed it with Darvula. The maid told her that indeed, many people believed that blood had special youth-giving properties for the complexion. Darvula then came up with a plan to "harvest" blood by holding young girls captive in the castle, as vampire expert Bob Curran explains:

> [Bathory] began to recruit young local girls from the villages round about, ostensibly to work as servants at Csejthe, but in reality to be murdered within the castle walls. Each day the Countess would bathe in their blood in the belief that it returned at least some of her youthful looks. There were accounts of her actually drinking the blood as a restorative medicine.[33]

In addition to many other cruelties, Vlad is known for impaling enemies and others who displeased him on sharp wooden stakes. Left to rot in the sun, the bodies served as a terrifying reminder of Vlad's power.

Porphyria

In the 1980s some suggested that there could be a medical cause of vampirism. It is a very rare genetic disorder called porphyria. People with this disease cannot adequately produce heme, a chemical component of the blood that carries oxygen throughout the body. Far more common in men than women, porphyria can cause symptoms that are often associated with vampires, including an extreme sensitivity to sunlight and a very pale or jaundiced complexion. In addition, many who suffer from porphyria often get a brownish red cast to their teeth.

In modern times people with porphyria can get injections of heme. However, some have suggested that people with porphyria who lived in earlier times might have had the urge to drink blood to satisfy a craving for heme. Though the idea was tantalizing for vampire historians, medical experts soon debunked the idea. They said that no one with porphyria would gain any relief from their condition by drinking blood.

A Gruesome Find

Though many young local girls went missing, authorities did little because most were from poor, peasant families. Rumors circulated, most likely thanks to workers within the castle, that many girls were being killed for their blood. In 1612 the king of Hungary, Matthias II, decided to intervene. He called for an official investigation.

What the investigators found was beyond belief. They found girls in various stages of being bled to death. They found one girl in the entryway of the castle who had been completely drained of blood, while others were penned up like animals, awaiting their turn to be bled.

The investigators found journals that Bathory had written, in which she listed the names of more than 600 victims. Darvula and other servants who had assisted in the murders were tried, found guilty, and beheaded. But because she was royalty, Countess Bathory was punished by confinement to her room for the rest of her life. Windows were walled with stones to keep all light out. The only connection she had with the outside world was a narrow slit in the door, where a plate of food could be sent in. It is not at all surprising that the name Elizabeth Bathory was detested from then on. In fact, say historians, after the revelation of her crimes, the name of her home, Csejthe, became a swear word in Hungarian.

Flesh-and-Blood Monsters

The stories of flesh-and-blood monsters such as Elizabeth Bathory and Vlad Dracula were frightening to all who heard them. Such stories fueled vampire beliefs and fears, as did ignorance of basic scientific processes. It is little wonder, then, that each new story of vampire attacks made the existence of vampires seem even more real than before.

Chapter 4

Vampires Among Us

Although fear of vampires was very strong in the past, it is much less of a concern in the modern age. The notion of bloodthirsty, foul-smelling, grave-dwelling killers stalking unsuspecting victims in the dark of night seems too improbable to be believed. However, the old fears and beliefs do resurface on occasion.

Vampires in the Jungle

One of the strangest examples took place in the Philippines during the mid-1950s. The CIA had special forces there, helping to keep President Ramón Magsaysay in power. Magsaysay was a staunch ally of the United States and was under attack by a Communist-backed group known as the Huks, who were trying to remove him forcibly from power. The Huks received the support of local Filipinos, which made the CIA's job more difficult.

Lieutenant Colonel Edward Lansdale was a key member of this CIA group. Lansdale learned that many of the Filipino people still believed in a vampire called an *aswang*, which supposedly targeted people with evil intentions. The *aswang* could shape-shift from a woman to a fierce bird that could pierce the neck of a human victim with its beak. Then it would leave the body hanging upside down in a tree, and all of the blood would drain away.

Lansdale's plan was to kill one of the Huks and make cuts on his neck to make it look as though he had been attacked by an *aswang*. Interestingly, the plan worked. When the soldier's body was discovered, the nearby villagers were horrified. Believing that the Huks were being targeted by vampires because of their evil intentions, the villagers stopped giving assistance to the Huk soldiers.

A New Kind of Vampire

The monstrous *aswang* vampire and others of its ilk have all but disappeared in the twenty-first century. Yet the idea of vampires is still very much alive—both in popular entertainment and in real life. However, this modern vampire is very much changed from its earlier counterpart.

In modern entertainment, vampires are often glamorous, sultry, and very appealing. This is Hollywood's touch. Actors like Brad Pitt and Tom Cruise have portrayed the vampire as a handsome, sympathetic figure. The modern Hollywood vampire is still feared, but not frightening. He can shape-shift by assuming the form of another human or an animal and move at incredible rates of speed from one place to another.

These more elegant vampires usually still depend on blood for sustenance, but instead of feeding on humans, they can exist on the blood of snakes, fish, lizards, and other small animals. Yet they still retain enough of their dark, mysterious ancestry to keep viewers on the edge of their seats.

Blending In

Self-described vampires today tend to keep a very low profile, not wanting to risk being ridiculed or discriminated against. Many say they rarely dress in vampire attire, except for when they attend special events. Most prefer that their vampire life remain private, so they dress, converse, and generally act like everyone else.

Linda Rabinowitz, a Virginia vampire, agrees wholeheartedly about laying low. She, too, breaks out the glitter only on very special occasions. A mother of a teenage son, she fits right into her suburban neighborhood. Dressing primarily in jeans and T-shirts, notes *Washington Post* reporter Monica Hesse, Rabinowitz is anything but frightening: "[She] radiates warm approachability. If you needed a quarter to get on the bus, she is the stranger you would ask."

Monica Hesse, "A Vampire's Life? It's Really Draining," *Washington Post*, November 24, 2008, p. C1.

"The Bad Boy in High School"

This type of vampire is very appealing to twenty-first-century readers, too. In the best-selling Twilight series, for example, author Stephenie Meyer spins a tale about a teen-age girl in small-town America who is in love with a vampire named Edward.

"He's more like the bad boy in high school, the kid your parents wouldn't let you go out with," says 58-year-old Trina, a fan of the Twilight series, who read the books after her granddaughter got hooked. "This vampire is a lot like the boy who smoked, who drove too fast, the good-looking one who gave your parents nightmares. But there was always an allure, you know? He was forbidden, but because he was supposed to be off limits, all the 'good girls' wanted to go out with him. I think it's that way for the modern vampire stuff."[34]

Twenty-one-year-old Isobel agrees. She says:

> The vampire isn't the villain, he's kind of like the misunderstood leading man in a movie. A lot of it is that the modern vampire isn't as bloodthirsty. He doesn't live in a coffin in the basement of a castle, he doesn't look like a monster. Actually, if you look at the old black-and-white movies and compare those vampires to the ones on TV now, there's very little similarity.[35]

Fangs and Glitter

At the same time that books, movies, and television have changed the image of vampires in the public imagination, a new type of vampire has surfaced in real life, too. A new vampire subculture has emerged in the United States, Europe, and other places around the world. This subculture exists on a couple of different levels.

For instance, thousands of people enjoy vampire role-playing games and going to clubs and bars with a vampire theme. There are dozens of clothing, jewelry, and accessory lines catering to young people who enjoy dressing the part, with black clothing, silver fang-shaped earrings, or striking blue or black glittery eye makeup.

Those who enjoy the role-playing and dressing up and the fun of assuming the character of a vampire are not the same as those who claim to be real vampires. "Basically, they are wannabes," says self-proclaimed vampire Patryck from New Jersey. "It's like kids dressing up for Halloween. I'm not criticizing them for having fun—in fact I know a couple of guys back East who really got deep into the dressing up part. One got fang implants—his dentist put them in. And the other guy ordered a set of wolf teeth off the Internet. They're like caps, you can take on and off, but they look real."

"But," Patryck adds, "just doing that kind of stuff doesn't really have anything to do with being a vampire. Vampirism is living a vampire lifestyle, and what your teeth look like or what you wear don't really count."[36]

"We're Not Monsters"

In fact, Patryck and others who describe themselves as twenty-first-century vampires say they are unlike any portrayals of vampires in fiction or history. "I'm not an expert, but I don't think there's much glamorous about it, like the movies are now," he says. "And at the same time, vampires aren't murderous and grotesque, as they were in old legends and folklore. We're not monsters. Really, it's a whole different world for vampires now."[37]

While modern vampires may be different from their predecessors in centuries past, they also share some rather unsettling characteristics that make them different from the average human being. The most important of these is a lack of a specific type of human energy they refer to as life force, or chi. As Scarlet, a self-described vampire who lives in Washington, D.C., explains, "I really look at my condition as more of an energy deficiency," she says. "I don't often produce enough energy to sustain myself."[38]

Patryck agrees, explaining that vampires do not use the word *energy* in the same way nonvampires do. "It's not just feeling tired or sleepy," he says. "It can be that, but like for me, I can't just get a good night's sleep and eat a healthy breakfast and get energy. Going to Starbucks won't help, either."[39]

Getting Energy from Others

What *does* help, vampires say, is sipping the energy from others, whom they call donors. The energy they require comes in two basic forms, and the type they require determines the type of vampire they are. The first type needs actual human blood to correct this energy deficiency. The second type is known as psychic vampires, and they feed off the emotional energy of other people without touching a drop of blood.

Either way, explains one vampire named Khan, replenishing that energy is a basic necessity for a vampire to live. "Our immune systems need the sustenance, just as a normal person might require the proper amount of vitamins and minerals." Both means contain the necessary chi, says Khan, "but the difference between taking in chi through psychic means versus blood consumption can be explained with a simple analogy: it's like the difference between drinking coffee or sucking on a coffee bean. The means of delivery

In the 1994 movie Interview with the Vampire, *actors Brad Pitt (left) and Tom Cruise portrayed their vampire characters as handsome and sympathetic figures. Similar treatment of vampires can be seen in other recent movies.*

is different. The concentration is different. But the contents are the same."[40]

Kris describes herself as a psychic vampire. She survives on emotional energy and says that there is no alternative for any true vampire—he or she has no recourse but to feed off others. "For us there is no pill, no therapy, no treatment— except to feed and to continue to feed. . . . We are seen as leeches, as wanton attackers, and as people doing this for the thrill. Few people understand that our need is like the need for food."[41]

"I Just Always Felt Tired"

Reezah, age 22, describes herself as a blood vampire. With numerous facial piercings, wearing a sweatshirt that reads "MY LIFE, NOT YOURS," she is a strikingly pretty young woman. She is also surprisingly soft-spoken—almost shy. She is neither proud of her vampirism nor ashamed of it. Being a vampire, she says, is simply who she is. Reezah explains:

> I grew up in Iowa on a farm. I was Elaine then—I haven't used that name in years. I never felt right growing up. Thinking back on my childhood, it was like I was waiting for something. I was bored all the time—I just always felt tired and kind of achy and flu-ish, like I was coming down with something. Nothing seemed to help, not lying down, not eating. It was just how I felt every day, it seemed like.
>
> And what I remember most about the farm was the loneliness, especially after my brother left for the Army. And the wind—it was constant, never stopped. I got so I wanted to scream, it was like listening to somebody whistling off-key all the time. If you've ever been on a farm, you know.[42]

But there was one aspect of her life on the farm that surprised her—an attraction to blood. "Not cruelty," she says quickly. "I wasn't a hunter, I wouldn't do that. But when my dad went out duck hunting in the fall, he'd bring back the ducks he shot in a plastic garbage can—a whole mess of them. I loved the smell of the blood. I wasn't afraid or grossed out to touch the blood, to taste it."[43]

Reezah says she had headaches a lot during her teens, and just thinking about blood and occasionally tasting it seemed to help lessen the severity of the headaches. "It could be my own blood, or the duck blood, it didn't seem to matter. I always wondered if there was something weird about me, or if other people felt that way. But it's not really something you could ask, or you'd get those looks. So I just did my blood thing, didn't tell anybody—ever."[44]

Awakening

Many people who claim to be vampires use the term *awakening* to explain the process of realizing their own vampirism. For some, awakening occurs in an instant; for others, it is a gradual process. Reezah says that her awakening occurred while at a friend's house when she was in high school:

> We were just sitting around, talking about a show we'd watched about vampires. I hadn't told her that I was attracted to blood. But I was thinking it would be interesting to try someone's blood, someone human. . . . At that point, I was trying to figure out how to bring it up without sounding stupid and weird. So I said, "I wonder how that would feel, being a vampire and drinking blood?" She said she thought it would be completely gross, but she kind of like dared me to try it.[45]

Reezah did try it. "And it was so weird. I tasted it, and made a face like it was horrible. That was hard, because I knew right away it was what I needed."[46]

Strange as It Sounds...

More people who claim to be vampires live in California than in any other state, according to a study by the Atlanta Vampire Alliance.

"What I Was Feeling Was Real"

Like Reezah, Patryck was unsure about why he always felt tired before his awakening. "I had all the medical tests," he says. "My parents thought I had mono, or was anemic. There was nothing wrong. I even got sent to a counselor, because my parents thought maybe I was making it all up to get out of going to school. I never cared about school much, but I wasn't making anything up. What I was feeling was real."[47]

Patryck enjoyed reading and liked the novels of author Anne Rice. "I thought about how maybe I was a vampire," he says. "I thought about how I was a night owl, never liked being outside in the sun, never went to the pool, just stayed inside most of the time. I guess all that made me start wondering about whether I could be a vampire—it seemed like a lot of the things I read about vampires could be said about me. Except the blood."[48]

He says that he considered the idea of experimenting with drinking blood, but rejected it quickly. He explains:

> The idea of drinking blood gagged me. But then I met a guy online who talked about how he was actually living a psi [psychic vampire] lifestyle. He sort of turned me on to the concept of tapping into energy, like from a crowd of people, or an exciting movie. That was exactly what worked for me. So I guess that's how I figured out that I was a psi, too. It explains a lot about me.[49]

Something Different

Best-selling author Michelle Belanger also describes herself as a psychic vampire. She says she knew early in life that

A young Iowa native who claims to be a vampire discovered a personal attraction to the smell of blood when she was young. She recalls wanting to touch and taste the blood of the ducks her father brought home from hunting trips.

there was something different about the way she interacted with other people's energy. She noticed it especially when she gave back rubs to high school friends in the band and choir:

> [I always knew] where to put my hands to relieve their tension and stress. It was not uncommon for people to fall asleep during one of my back massages, and everyone I massaged would comment on how I seemed to pull the tension out of them with my fingers. I had an instinctive understanding of where and how to use my hands, and I was always drawn right to the problem areas . . . as if I could somehow "see" inside them, perceiving muscle groups, damage, and swirls of light and dark energy.[50]

At the same time, she says, she had the sense that she was actually becoming more energized by taking their energy in. The more she tried, the better she became at tapping into other people's energy—a process vampires call "feeding." Over time she realized she could accomplish this merely by looking at the person and concentrating, without even touching him or her.

> On more than one occasion, I caught myself feeding unconsciously, daydreaming in class and focusing on the person in front of or across from me. One girl I did this to fell asleep at her desk, her head dropping down with an audible thump. Another student complained suddenly of feeling nauseated

The Black Veil

In 1999 Michelle Belanger, with the assistance of others in the vampire community, created a voluntary list of rules that they felt would serve as a code of ethics for modern vampires. They called their code the Black Veil. Some of the rules in the Black Veil deal with safety in feeding, as well as the need to remain nonviolent. "We are not monsters," says rule number four. "We are capable of rational thought and self-control. Celebrate the darkness and let it empower you, but never let it enslave your will."

The Black Veil also reminds vampires to be discrete about their lifestyle. Rule number one says:

> This lifestyle is private and sacred. Respect it as such. Do not make a sideshow of yourself. We do not have to prove ourselves to anyone. Appearing on public TV to tell the world that you drink blood is useless attention-getting. It gets a negative reaction for the whole community. Our place is in the shadows; our greatest protection from small-minded humanity is the fact that they do not believe we exist.

Quoted in Sanguinarius, "Thirteen Rules." www.sanguinarius.org.

and dizzy, asking to be excused so she could go to the infirmary.[51]

Feeding the Psi Vampire

Belanger learned that along with that special need of energy, she, like all vampires, must be careful and respectful. To continue to take energy from someone without that person's knowledge can be dangerous and unhealthy to that donor. Many modern-day vampires operate under a code of ethics called the Black Veil. This document contains strict rules about how vampires should conduct themselves, especially in how they feed.

For the psi vampire, that means being conscious about the source of the energy—for the sake of both donor and vampire. For Linda, a Virginia woman who says she is a vampire, that means not taking energy from people with drug or alcohol problems. "I stay away from people with medical issues," she says. "There's just too much complex emotion there." In addition, she is wary of donors she believes are not good people. "I try to stay away from people who are evil, basically,"[52] she says.

Forty-year-old Midnight says she feeds using her hands and her mouth. "I use my hands to initiate contact," she says, "and my mouth to 'breathe in' the energy."[53] Interestingly, although she does not come into contact with blood at all, she sometimes experiences the taste of blood in her mouth during a feeding—a phenomenon that she cannot explain. She explains the amazing feeling as the energy flows into her: "When I feed, I get a hot feeling in my hands that surges throughout my entire body as the feeding progresses. I can feel the energy that I am taking from my donor flow into my body and begin to disperse. Sometimes, although I am not [a blood vampire] I have had the coppery taste of blood in my mouth during feeding."[54]

She often uses her husband as a donor and says that the effects of her feeding from his energy vary from one feeding to the next. It seems to depend on how deeply she draws and how long the feeding lasts, she says:

> He has told me that when I feed he feels his en-
> ergy flowing out of him, and it is comparable
> to having a deep cut that bleeds profusely. He
> can actually feel his "life" draining out of him.
> He says it feels different from, for example,
> fighting sleep, as he can actually feel the drain
> taking place. I have noticed that my feeding is
> best done when my husband is sitting or lying
> down. I found out the hard way that initiating
> feeding while he was standing up landed him
> pretty quickly on the ground![55]

Dangers of Blood

Blood vampires, like psi vampires, require willing donors. "I've never heard of any blood vampire attacking people for blood—that's just in movies," says Reezah. "The way you do it is get a donor—or more than one—who you really trust."[56]

But many health-care workers say such a lifestyle is highly dangerous. With potentially fatal diseases like HIV/AIDS and hepatitis that are transmitted by blood, ingesting another person's blood poses a huge health risk. That is why donors need to be tested regularly for disease. Vampire Ravena advises others in the vampire community to be especially vigilant if they are blood vampires. "The 'I feel fine' method of testing is not acceptable," she stresses. "Get real lab work done."[57]

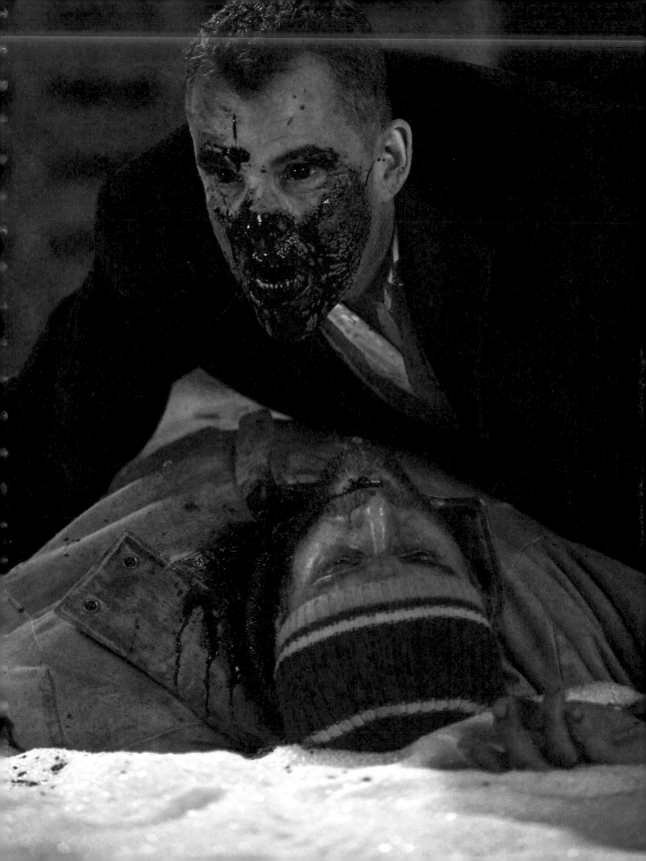

A Secretive Existence

Those who call themselves vampires in the modern age tend to live very secretive lives. They realize that most people cannot understand their way of life. SphynxCat, a self-proclaimed vampire who writes a Web page for fellow vampires, explains the need to keep their true selves hidden from the rest of the world:

> Real vampires, whether by nature or by circumstance, are often forced to live under a mantle of secrecy, and while that may sound very cloak-and-dagger, believe them when they say it's not all that fun or exciting. In many ways, it's, well, scary to tell someone about their vampirism (ever been made fun of? Multiply that times 100 and add a big dose of fear and superstition and you get the idea) for fear that whoever they tell won't believe them or will think they're a raving lunatic.[58]

But whether or not these modern-day humans who feel unwell unless they feed on another's blood or energy are actually vampires is a mystery. What is the way a vampire is measured? While there are similarities with the historical vampire, there are also jarring differences. They are not dead, nor do they attack humans. It is not clear whether there is anything magical or supernatural about these real-life vampires.

Others have suggested that modern vampires have evolved from their predecessors who rose from their graves to frighten and murder villagers. Is it possible that they really are the modern-day equivalent of those creatures? There is definitely a similarity to the secretive lifestyle and the aversion to being public about the way they feed. Did vampires ever exist? Do they exist now? It may be that no one will ever really know.

Source Notes

Introduction: Mercy's Grave

1. Bob Curran, *Vampires: A Field Guide to the Creatures That Stalk the Night.* Franklin Lakes, NJ: Career, 2005, p. 196.
2. Quoted in Rosemary Ellen Guiley, *The Encyclopedia of Vampires, Werewolves, and Other Monsters.* New York: Checkmark, 2005, p. 36.
3. Curran, *Vampires*, p. 198.

Chapter 1: Why Do People Believe in Vampires?

4. Bob Curran, *Encyclopedia of the Undead: A Field Guide to the Creatures That Cannot Rest in Peace.* Franklin Lakes, NJ: Career, 2006, p. 30.
5. Agnes Murgoci, "The Vampire in Romania," in Alan Dundes, ed., *The Vampire: A Casebook.* Madison, WI: University of Wisconsin Press, 1998, p. 33.
6. Quoted in Murgoci, "The Vampire in Romania," p. 33.
7. Ray Bhirk, personal interview with the author, September 14, 2009, Minneapolis, MN.
8. Quoted in Scribal Terror, "Capers of the Undead in Medieval England." http://scribalterror.blogs.com.
9. Quoted in G. David Keyworth, "Was the Vampire of the Eighteenth Century a Unique Type of Undead Corpse?" *Folklore*, December 2006, p. 241.
10. Quoted in Shroudeater, "William of Newburgh." www.shroudeater.com.
11. Quoted in Shroudeater, "William of Newburgh."
12. Quoted in Catholic Online, "Devil." www.catholic.org.
13. Quoted in Dudley Wright, *The Book of Vampires.* New York: Dorset, 1987, p. 23.

Chapter 2: Close Encounters

14. Quoted in Wayne Bartlett and Flavia Idriceanu, *Legends of Blood: The Vampire in History and Myth.* Westport, CT: Praeger, 2006, pp. 157–58.
15. Quoted in Olga Hoyt, *Lust for Blood: The Consuming Story of Vampires.* New York: Stein and Day, 1984, p. 93.
16. Hoyt, *Lust for Blood*, p. 95.
17. Hoyt, *Lust for Blood*, p. 102.
18. Quoted in Bartlett and Idriceanu, *Legends of Blood*, p. 14.
19. Quoted in Nocturnal Voices, "Visum et Repertum." www.nocturnalvoices.com.
20. Quoted in Nocturnal Voices, "Visum et Repertum."
21. Quoted in Nocturnal Voices, "Visum et Repertum."
22. Quoted in Hoyt, *Lust for Blood*, p. 106.
23. Quoted in Bartlett and Idriceanu, *Legends of Blood*, p. 23.
24. Quoted in Bartlett and Idriceanu, *Legends of Blood*, p. 24.
25. Quoted in Bartlett and Idriceanu, *Legends of Blood*, p. 24.

Chapter 3: Blood and Guts

26. Hoyt, *Lust for Blood*, p. 56.
27. Quoted in Paul Barber, *Vampires, Burial, and Death.* New Haven, CT: Yale University Press, 1988, p. 102.
28. Quoted in Bartlett and Idriceanu, *Legends of Blood*, p. 14.
29. Quoted in Barber, *Vampires, Burial, and Death*, p. 130.

30. Hoyt, *Lust for Blood*, p. 147.
31. Hoyt, *Lust for Blood*, pp. 64–65.
32. Quoted in Hoyt, *Lust for Blood*, p. 33.
33. Curran, *Encyclopedia of the Undead*, p. 73.

Chapter 4: Vampires Among Us

34. Trina, personal interview with the author, October 1, 2009, Minneapolis, MN.
35. Isobel, telephone interview with the author, September 14, 2009.
36. Patryck, personal interview with the author, October 3, 2009, Minneapolis, MN.
37. Patryck, interview.
38. Quoted in Monica Hesse, "A Vampire's Life? It's Really Draining," *Washington Post*, November 24, 2008, p. C1.
39. Patryck, interview.
40. Quoted in Michelle Belanger, ed., *Vampires in Their Own Words*. Woodbury, MN: Llewellyn, 2007, p. 80.
41. Quoted in Belanger, *Vampires in Their Own Words*, p. 4.
42. Reezah, personal interview with the author, October 2, 2009, Minneapolis, MN.
43. Reezah, interview.
44. Reezah, interview.
45. Reezah, interview.
46. Reezah, interview.
47. Patryck, interview.
48. Patryck, interview.
49. Patryck, interview.
50. Belanger, *Vampires in Their Own Words*, p. xiv.
51. Belanger, *Vampires in Their Own Words*, p. xvi.
52. Quoted in Hesse, "A Vampire's Life?" p. C1.
53. Quoted in Belanger, *Vampires in Their Own Words*, p. 11.
54. Quoted in Belanger, *Vampires in Their Own Words*, pp. 11–12.
55. Quoted in Belanger, *Vampires in Their Own Words*, p. 12.
56. Reezah, interview.
57. Quoted in Belanger, *Vampires in Their Own Words*, p. 98.
58. SphynxCat's Real Vampires Support Page, "Site Introduction." http://sphynxcatvp.nocturna.org.

For Further Exploration

Books

Michelle Belanger, ed., *Vampires in Their Own Words*. Woodbury, MN: Llewellyn, 2007.

Bob Curran, *Encyclopedia of the Undead: A Field Guide to the Creatures That Cannot Rest in Peace*. Franklin Lakes, NJ: Career, 2006.

Rosemary Ellen Guiley, *Vampires*. New York: Chelsea House, 2008.

Stuart A. Kallen, *Vampires*. San Diego, CA: ReferencePoint, 2008.

Barbara Karg, *The Everything Vampire Book*. Avon, MA: Adams Media, 2009.

Jay Stevenson, *The Complete Idiot's Guide to Vampires*. Indianapolis, IN: Alpha, 2009.

Web Sites

How Stuff Works: How Vampires Work (http://science.howstuffworks.com/vampire.htm). This is an excellent site, with a rundown of early Greek and Asian legends about vampires, information on modern vampires, and some of the reasons people found it so easy to believe in them.

Monstrous Vampires (http://vampires.monstrous.com). This site includes information on psi-vampires, blood vampires, and a number of famous vampires in history, including Elizabeth Bathory and Vlad Dracula.

The Psychic Vampire Resource and Support Pages (www.psivamp.org). This site includes information for people who are, or think they are, psychic vampires, as well as for people who are curious. Included is a YouTube interview with vampire author Michelle Belanger.

SphynxCat's Real Vampires Support Page (http://sphynxcatvp.nocturna.org). This site contains lots of links to items such as a glossary of terms, information on historical vampires, and interesting articles on bloodletting and blood-borne diseases. For new vampires or for people who think they might be vampires and want to learn more.

Vlad Dracula: The Truth (http://dracula-transylvania.blogspot.com). An entire site devoted to the life and activities of Vlad Dracula, with interesting links to his military campaigns, his castles, and what Romania was like in the Middle Ages.

Index

A

abchanchu, 10
Abhartach, 12–14
Allatius, Leo, 28–29
All Saints' Day, 23
*An Appeal to the Natural Faculties of the
        Mind of Man* (More), 28
appearance of vampires
        England, 22
        Greece, 22–23
        Malaysia, 10–11
        Romania, 18
        Scotland, 19
aswangs, 56–57
attacks, stopping. *See* prevention measures
Austria, 30, 32–33
awakening process, 64

B

Barber, Paul, 42–43, 45, 47
Bathory, Elizabeth, 49, 51–52, 55
Belanger, Michelle
        code of ethics for vampires, 68
        as psychic vampire, 65, 67, 69
        on vampires currently in New York City,
                8
Bhirk, Ray, 15–16
birth defects/differences, 20, 22
Black Veil, 68, 69
blessings after sneezing, 14
Blood Countess (Elizabeth Bathory), 49,
        51–52, 55
Bolivia, ancient, 10
books, 59
Brown family, 4–6, 8, 15
Buckinghamshire, England, 24–25
burials
        Christian rituals and, 23, 29–30, 38

disturbed grave sites, 46–47
measures to keep vampires in graves
        brick lodged between jaws, 26, 27
                (illustration)
        corpse upside down, 13, 46
        cross over grave, 28, 31 (illustration)
        head cut off, 28
        heavy object on grave, 13
        items to count near grave, 11
        quick, 12
        stake through vampire's heart, 18,
                25, 32, 44
        thorns around grave, 13
premature, 40–42

C

California, 64
Calmet, Augustin, 35, 37
catalepsy, 41–42
Cathain, 13
cauls, 20
characteristics of vampires, 10, 11, 38
Charles VI (emperor of Austria), 33
charms, 15, 36
chi, 61
chiang-shi, 12
China, ancient, 12
Christian Church
        burials and, 23, 29–30, 38
        condition of exhumed corpses and, 34
        measures to stop attacks
                cross over graves, 28, 31
                        (illustration)
                pardoning of sins, 25
        recognition of and reasons for vampires
                and, 21–22, 23, 33, 38
        vampire hysteria and, 30, 34–35, 38
corpses of vampires

burning and dismembering, 19, 21, 28, 29, 34

signs of vampirism

blood, 19–19, 32

bodies in apparent good health, 33–34

decomposition of bodies, 44–47

hair, nail, tooth growth, 32, 45

open left eye, 12

premature burials and, 40–42

stake through heart of, 18, 25, 32, 44

counting compulsion, 11

cross (Christian), 28, 31 (illustration), 37

Csejthe Castle, Hungary, 51, 52, 55

Cuntius, Johann, 42–43

Curran, Bob

on Bathory, 52

on burial of Abhartach, 13–14

on exhumation of Mercy Brown, 6, 8

on Mary Olive Brown, 5

D

Darvula, 52, 55

Davanzati, Giuseppe, 34–35, 37

decomposition of corpses, 44–47

dhampirs, 19, 21, 46

Diesel, Rudolf, 4

diseases

blood as transmitter of, 71

burials during plagues, 26

vampires as cause of, 4–6, 15–16, 18

Dissertation on Vampires, A (Davanzati), 34–35

dogs, 16, 22, 36, 42

donors, 69, 71

Dorko, 51

Dracul, Vlad, 47

Dracula (Stoker), 49

Dracula, Vlad, 47–49, 50 (illustration)

E

embalming, 42, 43 (illustration)

energy deficiency, 61–65

England

Buckinghamshire events, 24–25

dogs as vampires, 22

stake through heart outlawed, 25

York events, 16, 18–19

ethics code, 68, 69

excommunication, 23, 30

Exeter, Rhode Island, 4–6, 8

exhumations

Brown family, 6, 8

Medwegya vampire hysteria and, 33–34

in Romania, 40

eyes, false, 36

F

feeding process, 67, 69–70

fingerprinting, 4

fires, 36

Fluckinger, Johannes, 33–34, 44

folklore, 9–14, 19, 20

Fourth Lateran Council, 21–22

Fridays, 38

G

garlic, 32

Greece

appearance of vampires, 22–23

knocking on doors in Khíos, 28–29

Lamia in ancient, 10

Greek Orthodox Church, 23

Guiley, Rosemary Ellen, 20

H

hair growth, 32, 45

Halloween, 23

hepatitis, 71

Hesse, Monica, 58

History of the Events of England (William of Newburgh), 16, 18–19

HIV/AIDS, 71

Hoyt, Olga

on Bathory, 51

on Dracula, 48

on link between Church and vampirism, 30

on Medwegya events, 32–33

Huks, 56–57

hun, 12

Hungary, 46, 48, 51–52, 55

hunters of vampires, methods of, 17 (illustration), 19, 28

I

identification of vampires

    birth defects/differences, 20, 22

    blood flowing from corpses, 18–19, 32

    burials not soon after death, 12

    corpses in apparent good health, 33–34

    excommunication and, 23, 30

    hair, nail, tooth growth of corpses, 32, 45

    open left eye of corpses, 12

illnesses. *See* diseases

impaling bodies, 47–48, 53 (illustration)

India, 15

Innocent III (pope), 21

Interview with the Vampire (movie), 62 (illustration)

inventions, 4

Ireland, 12–14

Italy, 26

K

Khan, 61

Khíos, Greece, 28–29

knocking on doors, 28–29

Kris, 62

L

Lamia, 10

Lansdale, Edward, 56–57

laws, 39

Lazzaretto Nuovo, Venice, 26

life force, 61

Linda, 58, 69

M

Magsaysay, Ramón, 56

Malaysia, 10, 12

Map, Walter, 25, 28

Maria Theresa (empress of Austria-Hungary), 37–39

Matthias II (king of Hungary), 55

Medwegya, Austria, 30, 32–33

Metcalf, Harold, 6, 7, 8

Meyer, Stephenie, 59

Midnight, 69

modern vampires

    blending in, 58

    change in spelling of term, 57

    code of ethics for, 68, 69

    donors, 69, 71

    historical vampires compared to, 72

    in movies and books, 57, 59, 62 (illustration), 71 (illustration)

    population locations of, 8, 64

    types of, 61–65

    wannabes, 60

More, Henry, 28, 29

movies, 57, 62 (illustration), 71 (illustration)

Murgoci, Agnes, 14

N

Nadasdy, Francis, 51

nail growth, 32, 45

names for vampires, 10, 35

New York City, vampires in, 8

novels, 59

nuckelavees, 19

O

On the Current Opinions of Certain Greeks (Allatius), 28

P

p'ai, 12

Paole, Arnold, 30, 32, 44

Patryck, 60, 61, 65
penanggalan, 10, 12
Phantom World, The (Calmet), 35, 37
Philippines, 56–57
plagues
    burials during, 26
    vampires as cause of, 16, 18
porphyria, 54
prevention measures, 36
    burials with
        brick lodged between jaws, 26, 27
            (illustration)
        burning organs of corpses, 8
        corpses upside down, 13, 46
        cross over graves, 29, 31 (illustration)
        dismemberment of corpses, 21, 28
        items to count near grave, 11
        stake through vampire's heart, 19, 25,
            32, 44
    burning corpses, 19, 21, 29
    charms, 15
    garlic, 32
    thorns, 13, 36
Providence Journal (newspaper), 6
psychic (psi) vampires, 61–62, 65, 67, 69–70

R
Ravena, 71
Reezah, 63–64, 71
Rice, Anne, 65
Romania
    appearance of vampires in, 18
    birth defects, 22
    blessing after sneezing, 14
    Dracula, 47–49
    exhumation in, 40

S
Scarlet, 61
Scotland, 19
shapeshifting, 57

Silesia, 38, 42–43
silver weapons and religious objects, 36
sneezing, blessings after, 14
SphynxCat, 72
stake through vampire's heart, 18, 25, 32, 44
Stoker, Bram, 49
suicide, 25, 28
sunrise, 44
suspended animation, 41–44

T
30 Days of Night (movie), 71 (illustration)
tooth growth, 32, 45
tuberculosis, 15
Twilight series books, 59

U
unexplainable events, vampires as cause of,
    15

V
vampire bats, 35
vampire hysteria, 28–30, 32–33, 37–39
Vampires, Burial, and Death (Barber), 42–43
vampirism, described, 60
vampyres, 57
van Swieten, Gerhard, 38
Venice, Italy, 26
Virginia, 58

W
Washington Post (newspaper), 58
whitethorn, 36
William of Newburgh, 16, 18–19, 24–25
witchcraft, 51
wolves, 20

Y
yew trees, 13
York, England, 16, 18–19

About the Author

Gail B. Stewart is the author of more than 250 books for children and teens. The mother of three grown sons, Stewart lives in Minneapolis with her husband.